The Culinary Adventures of Augie J. Escoffier

The Way Better Peanut Butter Sandwich

Chef Ronald W. Shissler

PublishAmerica
Baltimore

First printing

ISBN: 9781462654338
PUBLISHED BY PUBLISHAMERICA, LLLP
www.publishamerica.com
Baltimore

Printed in the United States of America

Chef Shiss
12/2012

One day Augie J. Escoffier, a very bright child with a god given talent for all things chefy, decided for himself that he would make a sandwich.

Not just any sandwich, a sandwich in which he once tasted when his Grandmother Doris was alive. Grandma Doris was the one who discovered Augie's god given talent for all things chefy.

He remembered that the sandwich was between two slices of white bread and it tasted like peanut butter, but way better. It was in his lunch bag one day at school and he never had it again. Grandma Doris became an angel before she could make him another.

Augie asked his father. Do you know that peanut butter sandwich that grandma made for me at school? Dad said what did it taste like? It tasted like two slices of white bread and peanut butter, but way better. No son I don't know what you are talking about, then he gave Augie a big hug and off he went to work in the garden.

Augie asked his mother if she remembered the sandwich grandma made for him for his school lunch. What did it taste like sweetie? It tasted like two slices of white bread and peanut butter, but way better. No sweetheart, I only know her regular peanut butter sandwiches. Mother then gave Augie a big hug and off she went to garden in the yard.

Augie was confused, grown ups are suppose to know everything. I'll ask my little sister.

Augie found his little sister in her room playing with her giant sized dollhouse. Seanna, do you know that peanut butter sandwich that grandma made for me at school? Yes she made me one too said Seanna. Yeah! What was in it? I don't know I took one bite and it had chunky peanut butter and I traded it for a juice box, one cookie and a cupcake. In Augie's disappointment he yelled out darn!

Seanna suggested that Augie use his god given talent for all things chefy to invent the sandwich. Augie looked at Seanna and said yes I will put every food in the house between two slices of white bread with chunky peanut butter until I discover the sandwich again!

So the two began their journey in the kitchen while mother and father gardened outside.

Seanna found the bread and Augie grabbed the giant jar of peanut butter and they began their search. Augie started with the spices, he thought cinnamon would be it for sure! And it was not. Parsley? Nope, Oregano? Nope. Sage? Nope. Garlic? YUK! They went through all the herbs and none tasted like two slices of white bread and peanut butter, but way better.

Augie and his little sister spent hours looking through every food in the house. They had a stack of sandwiches that grew to the ceiling. Each sandwich filled with something between two slices of white bread and chunky peanut butter, candy, ham, cheese, carrots, jelly, peppers and so many things they ran out of bread.

Augie was very disappointed he looked at his little sister and began to wonder for the first time if he truly did have a god given talent for all things chefy.

Seanna looked around kitchen and realized what a mess there was. Seanna knew that this would not go well with mother and father who were outside gardening.

Just as Augie and his little sister began to clean up the kitchen mother and father walked in. Mother gasped and father yelled WHAT ARE YOU DOING?

Grape
Jelly

Augie stepped forward and said I was using my god given talents for all things chefy to find out what grandma put in her sandwich that tasted like two slices of white bread and peanut butter, but way better.

Mother told Augie that grandmother only made one kind of peanut butter sandwich. When Grandma Doris was a child people ground their own peanuts into peanut butter. Sugar was very hard to find sometimes, so peanut butter did not have sugar added to it like the store bought peanut butters of today. Grandma didn't know about the store bought peanut butters, so every time she made peanut butter sandwiches she added a little brown sugar to the top of it. And that is all.

Augie was very happy to find out what grandmother had put in her sandwiches and angry because it was brown sugar he was holding in his hand when they ran out of bread.

Grape
Jelly

That night mother went to the store to buy bread while father, Seanna and Augie cleaned up the kitchen. They fed the sandwiches to their farm animals that ate every thing except the garlic one. Once they had finished mother made Grandma Doris's sandwiches and she grilled them, which made them even way better.

Ever since that day and every now and then mother made Grandma Doris's peanut butter and brown sugar sandwiches for Augie and Seanna's school lunches. Augie ate every crumb and Seanna traded them away for anything worthy of such a treat. Everyone would ask them if they knew how to make those sandwiches that tasted like two slices of white bread and peanut butter, but way better. And they knew.

Recipe

The Way Better Peanut Butter Sandwich
2 Slices of Bread (any kind will do)
4 Tablespoons of Peanut Butter (chunky or smooth it's all up to you)
1 Tablespoon of Brown Sugar
1 Paper plate
1 Butter knife

Gather all your tools and ingredients and have them all in their place.
Place the bread open on your paper plate.
Apply 2 tablespoons of peanut butter to each slice of the bread.
Sprinkle the brown sugar over the peanut butter on only one slice then smash the two sides together and cut off the crust.

If you want to make this even way better...
Spread 1 tablespoon of butter on both sides of the bread
Then grill in a frying pan until golden brown on both sides.
The Grilled way better peanut butter sandwich.